HARMONIES ABROAD

YALE GLEE CLUB'S POST-WWII ODESSY OF EUROPE IN 1949

GEORGE PRATT

Copyright © 2024 by George Pratt

All rights reserved.

ISBN

Print 978-1-63777-686-5

Digital 978-1-63777-685-8

No part of this book may be reproduced in any form or by any electronic or mechanical means, including information storage and retrieval systems, without written permission from the author, except for the use of brief quotations in a book review.

CONTENTS

Book 1949 tour	1
Preparation	5
The Trip Begins	8
The Netherlands	15
Denmark	18
Sweden	21
Finland	26
Norway	31
Germany	39
The Trip Home	49
Retrospection	52
Appendix	55
Acknowledgments	57
About the Author	59

father-in-law was the director of the glee club at Connecticut College for Women, and I think we did a joint concert with them of Brahms Requiem.

Choral singing became important to me. I realized that my musical skills were above average. I could read music well, and my ear for the correct tones was quite accurate. But I also realized that my singing voice was not so good. Because I seriously wanted to be accepted into the Yale Glee Club in my junior year, I took voice lessons over the summer vacation.

They paid off! For I was one of the two juniors who were accepted. The other was Steven Harbacheck who had a beautiful baritone voice. He later continued his career in opera.

Marshall Bartholomew was director of the Yale Glee Club. Everyone called him "Barty." He was the leader of the international association of choral singers and was welcomed all over the world. Many of his arrangements had been published.

I recall that at our first rehearsal in the Fall, Barty handed out some music, explaining that twenty years earlier, in 1928, he had accepted a friend's invitation to visit him in North Carolina over the Easter holiday. The friend knew of a small black church that performed some excellent spirituals. Barty's hobby was collecting and arranging spirituals and folk songs. They went to the church and Barty made notes in his musical shorthand of two of the songs. When he came back to New Haven, he put one of the songs in the back of his desk drawer, and arranged the other song, "Humble in my Soul." His arrangement was published and became a staple in the Glee Club's repertoire.

Last Summer, twenty years later according to Barty, he was cleaning his desk and found his notes of the other song tucked away in the back. He arranged it, calling it "Lil Innocent Lamb" and now wanted the Glee Club to try it out. Our first performance of the new spiritual was at the joint Harvard-Yale concert, the night before the "Big Game." When we finished singing it, a packed house in Woolsey Hall leaped to its feet cheering "More!

More!" We had to sing it again, and it has been a glee club favorite ever since.

The Fall semester was, for the Glee Club, rather routine. We prepared for and took a Christmas tour in the Midwest and had several local concerts. When we returned to school for the New Year, however, Barty stunned us with an announcement.

PREPARATION

At our first rehearsal after the Christmas break, Barty announced that he had arranged for the Glee Club to make a summer tour of Scandinavia and Germany. We would be singing in the four Scandinavian countries over four weeks and then spend two weeks in Germany, sponsored by the U. S. Government. Excitement was high, but Barty cautioned us that Europe, and especially Germany, had not fully recovered from the damages of war and their facilities were not yet able to accommodate many tourists. So there had to be a limit on how many members in the Glee Club could go along. The traveling group would be selected later in the spring.

In the meantime, we would have to prepare our program, which would include some of the songs we were familiar with, but also some new songs, one of which was being written by Paul Hindemith, a visiting composer to the music school. It was called "Demon of the Gibbet." Barty stressed how honored we should be that a great composer like Hindemith would dedicate one of his creations to the Glee Club

Sometime in April, Barty announced who would be making the

trip. Surprisingly, Steve Haarbacheck and I, the two juniors in the club, were also included. The reason for Steve was obvious. He had the best singing voice in the entire group. It may be that I was included because I had recently been elected President of the Glee Club for the following year. Whatever the reason, I was delighted that I made it on the list.

Barty continually reminded us that when on tour outside the United States we always have to keep in mind that we are ambassadors of goodwill, representing our country. He also cautioned us when abroad, never to sing the Yale Alma Mater, "Bright College Years," because its tune had been adopted by the Nazis as the Nazi national anthem. At that time, so close after the war, singing that song might set off a riot, and it would certainly be offensive to most Europeans.

Barty explained that the tour would be divided in two parts, the first part being four weeks in England, France, the Netherlands, and Scandinavia, and the second part, two weeks, in Germany, paid for and directed by our government, which was hoping to spread goodwill among the universities of Germany. We were to travel by train from one university town to the next, and spend the day and evening fraternizing with and singing to the students.

Our clothing was also divided in two parts. We were to take with us two bags. One was to contain our traditional formal dress of white tie and tails. After our concerts in England, Paris, and the Netherlands, we would ship our formal bag home and continue on with only the prescribed informal dress, which was to consist of a blue blazer, gray flannels and one pair of sun tan pants, plus two pair of blue socks, and two-each of under pants, under shirts, white button-down shirts, and blue neckties. We were told that laundry facilities would not be available, so the socks, underwear, shirts, and ties would all be made of nylon. They could be easily washed out and quickly dried for re-use.

We were also told that electricity would be unreliable, so we should not plan to rely on our electric shavers. For seven years I had been using only an electric shaver, so I decided to buy shaving cream and a safety razor for the trip. To my surprise, I found the safety razor much better than the electric one, and have continued to use it for 74 years thereafter.

To the list of permitted items, I mentally added two cartons of Chesterfield cigarettes. I did not smoke, but I had heard that in Europe, especially Germany, American cigarettes were highly prized. I thought they might come in handy as a type of currency.

As our departure day grew closer, Paul Hindemith came to two of our rehearsals and led us through his new composition. What an experience!

I do not recall the full program we sang for the trip, but I do know that it included, in addition to Norwegian composer Edward Grieg's "Brothers Sing On" and Hindemith's "Demon of the Gibbet," a novelty song, "O Tremsino" by Villa Lobos, a Madrigal Group of eight Glee Club singers, who performed four or five old English madrigals. We wound up each concert with a group of spirituals such as "Little Innocent Lamb," and traditional Yale songs – "Aura Lee," "Winds of Night," "Bulldog," "Careless Love," "Mother of Men," and "A Song for Old Yale."

Barty had persuaded Juan Trippe, CEO of Pan American Airlines and a member of Yale's governing body, the Yale Corporation, to provide the entire Glee Club with round-trip air transport to and from Europe at a steep discount.

THE TRIP BEGINS

On June 21, 1949, soon after we had sung for Yale's Commencement Concert, we all gathered at Idlewild airport (now JFK) and boarded the civilian version of the B-29 bomber, which was our chartered means of travel to Europe.

Idlewild Airport - Ready to take off

This was my first airplane trip, so I came armored with plenty of

Dramamine, to counter any air sickness I might be plagued with. Fortunately, I survived the trip with no problems.

Our propeller-driven airliner had to stop twice to refuel. The first stop was at Gander, Newfoundland. It was dark and we could not see much. The second stop was at Shannon, Ireland. It was early morning, and we enjoyed the panoramic views of the Irish countryside.

The last leg brought us to England. London was covered by dense clouds and our pilot was instructed to circle above the clouds until called in. As we circled for about a half hour in the bright sunlight above the clouds, peering out of our windows we could see six or seven other air liners also circling. Every once in a while a plane would disappear into the dark clouds, presumably heading for a safe landing at Heathrow Airport.

Finally, it was our turn to drop into the dark clouds. It was, for me on my first flight, a scary experience. I could not help but wonder if we would crash into the ground. Eventually, we came out of the cloud bank, and the ground was only about 300 feet below us. Contrary to my fears, the pilot had us under control and he deftly guided us into a landing ramp at Heathrow.

After clearing customs and collecting our luggage, two buses transported our crowd of 65 to a hotel in downtown London, located near Kingsway Hall where our London concert was to be presented. First, however, we had a broadcast at BBC Studios. It was interesting to see the relaxed, informal approach of the announcer. He paid no attention to the clock, and at about five minutes after the hour, immediately following a news item, he casually switched to a conversational, "We are fortunate to have with us this evening, a singing group from the States, the Yale Glee Club, directed by Marshall Bartholomew, which is beginning a six-week concert tour of Europe and Germany. Let's hear how they sound." We followed that with four or five of the songs for our tour.

Much of London had been rebuilt after the bombing, but here and there we could see entire blocks of rubble that had not yet been fixed up.

The next day we traveled to Oxford University, where we were to present our second concert.

Oxford

The students there had already gone home for the summer recess, so we were allowed to spend the night in one of their dormitories. Facilities for students at Oxford didn't begin to compare with what we were used to at Yale. Instead of individual bathrooms with showers, their bathroom was a large communal room with a few showers and lengthy open urinals along the walls.

Our concert went well that evening, although the audience seemed to be a little cold, unresponsive. The next morning we boarded our buses and headed back to London to give our concert at Kingsway Hall, a major musical venue. The audience there, too, was a little cold and unresponsive.

The next morning, we boarded buses to take us South, to Dover, where we got on a ship to traverse a rough English Channel to Calais in France. We were to spend three days in Paris with only a single concert on the last evening at the Sorbonne, one of the premier universities in France.

Paris

The only thing I recall about the concert was that the concert hall was on the second floor, and the audience did not clap to show their appreciation but instead they stamped their feet on the floor. We had not been alerted to this custom and when we concluded our opening number, Grieg's "Brothers Sing On," the booming noise of the stamping feet startled us. It sounded like the building was falling down.

During the days of our Paris visit, we were treated to various tours and visits to the principal tourist places –the Louvre, the Eiffel Tour, Notre Dame Cathedral, Versailles.

At the Louvre, I was not impressed by the Mona Lisa, but walking up a long, wide stairway I was totally captivated by the statue of the Winged Victory of Samothrace. Never before had a work of art reached into my soul.

At Versailles, before exploring its mirrored halls, we gave an outdoor concert in its large courtyard. The many people there, tourists and natives alike, enthusiastically received our efforts. For this event we were led by Wally Collins, the Assistant Director for the tour. Most of the singers felt that he did a fairly poor job. Of course, anyone playing second fiddle to Barty would never be acceptable to the chorus, and Wally was not asked to substitute for Barty at any time later in the tour.

Wally had been a member of the Glee Club two or three years earlier, and was working as the director of music in a New England prep school. Barty brought him along on the tour specifically to serve as Assistant Director. Of course, his excellent first-tenor singing voice was a welcome addition.

The next year, Barty announced his retirement and the beginning of a search for a replacement. Barty had been the fourth director in the hundred years since the Yale Glee Club had been formed. When the search came down to a choice between Wally Collins and Fenno Heath, a group of us went to Barty to try to convince him to choose Fenno. One of our arguments was Wally's poor performance in the Versailles courtyard. Fenno was ultimately chosen, and he served as Director of the Yale Glee Club for many years. He also adeptly handled the conversion from an all-male chorus to a mixed chorus when Yale decided to go co-ed in 1976.

We had two evenings free in Paris before our concert at the Sorbonne. Many of us had heard about the loose morals of the French, and a few of us decided to go exploring. We headed for Pigalle and walked up a dimly lit street to a nightclub, called the Bal Tabarin. We went in to verify the rumor that French dancers perform topless. They did! But the price was so expensive. A small glass of Coke cost 'two mille francs', about ten dollars in American currency, so we decided to leave.

Outside in the warm summer evening our steps turned to the right, along another dimly lit street that seemed to have an unusual number of women. We assumed they were prostitutes, and when one of them approached the three of us and asked in French, 'Mille francs?' We were so startled that we could do no more than politely decline.

From there, we continued up the hill to a cross street, at the end of which we thought we could see the famous cathedral Sacre Coeur.

Sacre Coeur

As we drew closer, we could hear some choral singing. Through a side door we crept into the large sanctuary, at the front of which was a men's choir obviously rehearsing for an upcoming service. In the empty auditorium, the reverberations enhanced the sound to a beautiful blend of the voices. We listened carefully for a few minutes and then retreated through our entrance door, feeling refreshed by those angelic voices.

The next evening, a number of the men decided to go out exploring again. I felt a little tired, so I stayed behind in the lobby of our hotel. Soon, an attractive young lady about my age walked into the lobby and sat in a lounge chair. When she smiled at me, I said, "Bonsoir." She said she was German and spoke no English, but she did know a little French. I told her I spoke no German, but also could handle a little French. She invited me to sit next to her, and we spent a delightful evening conversing about Paris, life and other things, all in our fractured French. I found the evening far more enjoyable than walking the streets of Paris.

After the Sorbonne concert we were all taken to the Gare du Nord, to board a train that would end our Paris visit and move us north into the Netherlands.

THE NETHERLANDS

We arrived in Amsterdam at around noon. After checking into our hotel, we were treated to a boat tour of the city. My strongest memory of that tour was a vision of a house that was only four feet wide, crammed in between two larger buildings. Of course there were lots of poppies.

Holland

That night we sang our concert at the Concertgebouw, Amsterdam's most prominent concert hall. We had little contact with the Dutch people and seemed to be constantly on the move. The next morning we all gathered at the bus station to begin our trip north to Groningen.

Barty met us there and distributed some music. He said that in Groningen we were doing a command performance for Princess Juliana. The music was the Dutch National Anthem that we would sing for her. Barty said that the Glee Club would rehearse the anthem and learn the pronunciations on the two buses while on the drive up along the dike that creates the Zuider Zee. He said that I, as the Baggage Master for the tour, would have to ride along in the truck carrying the group's 130 bags. With that we loaded into our respective vehicles and began the trip to the north, with the two buses leading the way and our truck following.

My truck driver didn't speak either English or French, so there was no conversation as we rode along. Then I remembered the Dutch National Anthem and retrieved it from my pocket. As I hummed the tune the driver became interested and, realizing what I was doing, he began to sing along with me, coaching me on the difficult pronunciations.

At Groningen we were all treated to lunch and then led into the concert hall for rehearsal. Barty led us through our program and then explained that our host for the day was a former Yale Glee Club member who was now the US Ambassador to the Netherlands. Barty said he had requested the privilege of leading the chorus in the National Anthem. We clapped a welcome for him as he stood in front of the chorus and started us into the National Anthem. Full of confidence from the truck Driver's teaching on the trip up from Amsterdam, I sang out loudly, hoping to help some of my buddies with the words. Our director stopped us and pointed at me, "Young man, where did you learn that?"

"From the truck driver, on the trip up."

"Well, there is something you should know. In English there is the King's English and the Cockney English. The truck driver has taught you the Cockney Dutch. Please sing softly."

Properly chastised, I barely made a sound that night. Especially appreciated by the audience was our rendition of their National Anthem. This was only four years after the end of the war and the Nazi occupation, and feelings of patriotism were running high.

The rest of the concert went off well and the next day we traveled to The Hague for our main Dutch concert at Ridderzaal Hall.

The following day we returned to Amsterdam and met at the railroad station, where we all deposited our suitcases with the formal attire and addressed each bag to be sent back to our respective homes. From here on we were going to be limited to our nylon clothes, blue blazers and gray flannels.

DENMARK

Our train from Amsterdam took us across an attractive rural landscape in northern Germany and brought us into Copenhagen, Denmark, in the early hours of the afternoon.

Copenhagen did not show any war damage, for Denmark's tiny army was no match for Hitler's Wehrmacht and the country immediately surrendered at the start of World War II in 1939. Capitulation by the military did not, however, complete a surrender by the population. Throughout the war the Danish underground resistance managed to harass the occupying forces and to relay intelligence information to the western forces. The man who led Denmark's resistance was now a prominent businessman in Copenhagen. That same man, whose name I cannot recall, served as host to the Glee Club on our short stay there.

He made all the arrangements for us, including our concert in a glass-enclosed concert hall in Tivoli Gardens, a famous entertainment/amusement park in the center of the city. After the concert, he led us on foot for a couple of blocks to one of Copenhagen's swankiest night clubs. It had been closed for the summer recess, but he used his influence to open it and welcome the singing visitors from America. And he did far more than that. He arranged a full banquet and drinks for us at 10pm that evening.

Best of all, he had persuaded 60 young ladies from a local college to join us for the evening. They all spoke English and they enthusiastically joined us to celebrate our coming to Denmark. There was plenty of food, drink, and singing. The merrymaking went on well after midnight.

The next morning, he joined us at the waterfront to wish us well on our next stop in Sweden and for the remainder of our Scandinavian concert tour. We boarded a ship bound for Gothenburg, Sweden. I remember as we departed Copenhagen harbor, we passed rather close to the statue of the mermaid, which is a symbol of Denmark,

Copenhagen, Denmark – The Mermaid

but I remember nothing else of the boat trip except that the scenery along the Swedish coast was gorgeous. I cannot recall anything about Gothenburg – our concert there, or the next day's trip across Sweden to Stockholm, even whether it was by train or bus.

Gothenburg

SWEDEN

Stockholm, in contrast, produced several memories. It is a city built on seven islands and is sometimes referred to as "Venice of the North." Sweden remained neutral during the War, so it had suffered no damage. Post-war it emerged as one of the most prosperous countries in Europe.

We arrived on July 4th, and our concert was in a large concert hall located in a setting similar to Copenhagen's Tivoli Gardens. The Glee Club was part of a celebration given by the city to honor the local Americans, of whom there were many. Among them was a twenty-year-old girl, a blue-eyed blonde named Kitty Kolb, who took a shine to me. (Maybe it was the other way around.)

Anyway, she had come to the concert as part of the July 4th festivities. She had been living in Stockholm for two or three years while her dad was completing a special part of his job there. They lived in New Jersey, and would be returning soon. At ten o'clock after the concert, in that far-north location, it was still daylight, so she showed me around some of the sights of the city. As I walked her home at 1am I shared my surprise that there was still enough light to read a newspaper. The next morning she came down to the wharf to see us off on our short boat trip to Visby, on the Swedish island of Gotland, and she promised to meet us when we returned two days later.

Gotland was a beautiful place, lush with roses. The city of Visby had eighteen churches, all but one of which was in ruins, having been repeatedly sacked over the centuries by the many invading forces that had sequentially conquered this island since the Middle Ages. The island was situated at a crucial point on the trade route between the Baltic Sea and the North Sea, and was a favorite port for ships of the Hanseatic League, plying their goods to and from Norway, Great Britain, France and beyond. More recently, it had become a favorite resort area for vacationing Swedes.

Our concert was in the only building in Visby large enough to accommodate us and an audience – the one remaining church, called the Cathedral of St. Mary, which was like a giant echo chamber inside.

Visby – Cathedral of St. Mary - outside

Cathedral al of St. Mary – inside

At our afternoon rehearsal we soon discovered that the reverberations of our voices continued so long that singing a fast number, such as Little Innocent Lamb, was impossible. It simply created a lot of noise, as the projection of one note competed with the echoes from the two previous notes. Barty decided on the spot that we had to change the program we had been singing up to that point. He kept the few slow numbers on the program, and reached back to the list of 36 Yale songs that all Glee Clubbers were expected to memorize, and found several that could survive the echoing onslaught. He also chose a couple of slow numbers that had been part of the program that many in the Chorus had sung the previous year.

Needless to say, it was a long and difficult rehearsal, for we had severe trepidations about the upcoming evening concert. Contrary to our fears, however, we were a smash hit! The people truly enjoyed it. But you could not tell by the applause, for there was none. The rules of the cathedral barred any clapping of hands or cheers. They did allow an audience to wave their programs to express their appreciation of a song. After each number we could see the white programs being vigorously flapped back and forth, and after it was over, outside the cathedral several members of the audience went out of their way to tell us how much they had appreciated our performance.

Early the next morning we took the boat back to Stockholm for a full day of sight-seeing and relaxation. Kitty met us, as promised, and served as a tour guide during the day for me and a few envious friends.

After a late supper Kitty asked me if I would like to see the Royal Palace, which was just across the water from the downtown area we were in. Boats ran on schedules, like buses, in this city of islands. Kitty selected the proper "bus" to the King's island. When we got there, she led me through a small commercial area near the wharf to a winding road that led uphill for nearly a half a mile toward the looming palace.

Stockholm – The Royal Palace

Kitty mentioned that she was getting cold. I quickly offered her my blazer to keep her comfortable. When the road leveled out there was a large area like a parking lot, with the Palace entrance off to the right.

No one was to be seen and there were no lights on in the palace. Of course, despite the late hour we could still see our way along. Kitty suggested that we walk straight ahead to the edge of the parking area. We stopped at a small wall and right in front of us was a panoramic view of Stockholm. As we stood there admiring the sight and discussing it, we heard a rough male voice speaking in Swedish. I turned and saw a soldier standing close to us, with his machine gun leveled at our heads.

I gasped, but Kitty spoke softly to him. She then turned to me and whispered, "We are not supposed to be here, but it will be OK if we leave — right now!" We quickly made tracks down the winding road and happily caught the next "bus" back to the downtown area.

The next morning Kitty again came down to the wharf to see us off on the boat to Turku, Finland. We exchanged mailing addresses and she wished me well on the rest of our tour.

Digression: Later on, we carried on a correspondence that continued throughout the school year. After she and her family returned to New Jersey, sometime around June, she wrote that she would be visiting some relatives for a weekend at Keuka Lake, where I had spent all of my summers. She wondered if we might get together there.

Of course! I thought it would be great to see her, and it would give me a chance to reciprocate and serve as a tour guide for her. The weekend at Keuka Lake went well, but it was too short. A few weeks later, back at law school, I invited her to Yale for a football weekend, once again playing the role of a tour guide. Somehow, however, things were different between us. We just didn't click as we had in Stockholm's fairyland. She thanked me for the weekend, and I never saw her again.

FINLAND

<u>Back to the tour.</u> Our seagoing trip to Turku began with about two hours of weaving our ship through a variety of islands, heading eastward. Called by the dinner bell, we all headed for the glassed-in dining room where a sumptuous Smorgasbord was laid out for us. We lined up and loaded our plates with the tempting food.

About half-way through the line, I noticed that our ship had left the islands, and we were now in the open waters of the Baltic Sea. Struggling against a strong quartering head-wind and large waves, it was sometimes difficult to keep my balance as the ship pitched. I was able to finish loading my plate and I carefully made my way to sit at a table with other Glee Clubbers.

As I pulled out my chair to sit down, I suddenly felt nauseous. I set down my plate and quickly made my way back to my cabin, swallowed two tablets of Dramamine, which someone had urged me to bring on the trip in case of seasickness, and I lay down on my bed to let my stomach calm down.

The next thing I was aware of was the sound of men singing. I opened my eyes. It was morning, and I was still dressed in my clothes from yesterday. The singing came from the Turku University Chorus, which had come down to the harbor at 6:00 am to welcome the Yale Glee Club to Turku as its ship pulled into port.

Turku – Waterfront

The Turku University Glee Club, like the choruses of many universities in Europe at that time, was locally centered. Most of its students came from the immediate locality, and after graduation they lived and worked in the same area. The glee clubs then tended to retain the good singers after they had graduated, and the majority of those we saw that day were middle-aged men, but enthusiastic and excellent singers.

We had looked forward to the highlight of our day in Turku, which was to be a visit with Jean Sibelius, the famous Finnish composer and a friend of Barty's. When we arrived that morning, however, we were told that Sibelius was sick and would not be able to meet with us. A great disappointment. After the concert that evening, the Turku chorus entertained us for dinner and a long evening of eating, drinking, and singing together.

Turku – Orthodox church

The next day we boarded a train for the trip south to Helsinki, the capital of Finland. On the train someone explained to us that Russia had started a war with Finland back in the 1930's, which of course we knew. What we didn't know was that one result of the war was that Russia had commandeered a ten-mile-wide strip of Finnish land, that led from Russian territory to the Baltic Sea. It gave Russia's navy access to the Baltic, and thence through the North Sea to the Atlantic Ocean.

The reason for the history lesson was that our train had to cross this strip of Russian territory. We were told that when we reached there, the train would stop, the windows would be boarded up, the Finnish engine would be replaced by a Russian one, and the Finnish train crew would be replaced by Russians. During the trip across those ten miles, we were warned not to make any disturbance or get into any arguments with the Russians.

It all happened as predicted, except that half-way through, the train stopped. We peered through the cracks in the boards over the windows and saw that we were at some kind of military base. Bill Coffin, our President, had been a liaison officer between the US and

Russian armies at the end of the War, and had spent many nights drinking and singing with his Russian counterparts. Steve Harbichek, our baritone soloist, was a native-born Russian, and he and Bill had already on many occasions entertained the rest of the Glee Club with duets of Russian folk songs.

Soon after we had stopped, Bill and Steve went into the vestibule of their car and began singing the Russian folksongs. Soldiers quickly gathered outside the car and would cheer them on after each song. But then, an officer appeared, and the soldiers quickly dispersed, ending the impromptu concert. With that, the train moved on and when we reached the point where the tracks reentered Finnish territory, the train stopped. The boards were removed from the windows, the Russian engine and crew were replaced, and the train then continued on to Helsinki.

Our time in Helsinki was just one day. We felt none of the warmth and spirit there that we had experienced in Turku. After the concert we did have a party at the Helsinki Yacht Club, located on an island in the harbor, and it provided us a great view of the lighted city.

Helsinki

Helsinki – The University

The only memory I have of the party is that, as usual, as we sat at our tables after dinner, Barty led us in several songs to further entertain the locals. With many of my singing colleagues well lubricated by the schnaps that kept filling our glasses, we all enjoyed singing from our tables the usual Yale Songs and Spirituals. T

Then Barty called out the name of a song, which I didn't hear. He blew his pitch pipe to set the key, and started to sing while he was conducting. He had a solo, because no one in the Glee Club had ever heard of the song. Maybe Barty, too, had a little too many schnaps.

NORWAY

From Helsinki, we traveled by boat west to Oslo, Norway. On our arrival we were taken directly to a building with a large auditorium. Barty asked us to be seated. He explained that our Oslo supervisor had arranged with people living locally to take us into their homes, rather than have the expense of providing a hotel for us.

Oslo

Oslo

The Supervisor then confirmed this and said that each host would be responsible for a pair of choristers each during our stay in Oslo. They would provide us lunch and see to it that we get to the concert, give us a place to sleep tonight, and provide us breakfast the following day. This was a welcome change from the parade of hotels and hostels that we had so far experienced.

When my name was called, along with another singer whose name I do not recall, we went forward and were presented to an attractive young woman, in her late teens, who introduced herself, in very good English, as Annalise Brondmo. She took us to her home, and over lunch prepared by her mother, mentioned that beginning in September she was traveling to Philadelphia to work there for her uncle. She had signed up as a hostess for the Glee Club so as to give her a chance to practice her English. After lunch she invited us to go swimming. We both happened to have bathing suits. "I'll bring the towels," she said. "Follow me," and we walked to a nearby beach.

Not too many people were swimming that day. My friend and I looked around for a bath house or somewhere we could change into our bathing suits, but there were no structures in sight. Annalise led us to a suitable spot near the water. She sat down and spread a towel over her body and began changing into her bathing suit. I was somewhat shocked. I had never seen this done before, but I thought,

"When in Rome, do as the Romans do." So I, too, sat and covered myself with my towel, and started changing as if it were the most natural thing in the world.

After our swim, Annalise arranged for a taxi. She said that the American Ambassador was giving a pre-concert cocktail party and we should be there at about 4:00. When we pulled up at the gate to the Embassy, she said she would meet us there at 6:00 to take us to the concert hall.

We asked, "Aren't you coming with us?"

"Oh, no," she replied. "They told us distinctly that the party was only for the Americans."

"Ridiculous," we answered. "If you don't come, we won't go, and you will have failed in your mission to get us there."

Annalise reluctantly entered the Embassy with us and we all enjoyed the party, especially because every member of the Glee Club had the same response we had and insisted that their hosts join them. The Ambassador who planned that event did not have much sense for how to deal properly with people. These people were extending themselves personally and financially in taking care of us and sharing their still-rationed food. They deserved at the very least, the respect of sharing that embassy party. I still feel glad that the Yale Glee Club proved to be better ambassadors than the professionals had been.

The evening's concert was followed by dinner and a party, to both of which, thankfully, our hosts were invited and attended. We stayed overnight at Annalise's house and in the morning were treated to a fine American breakfast of bacon and eggs. We learned later that as a result of the war, food was still rationed in Norway, and that the breakfast we had probably cost the Brondmo family at least two weeks of food stamps. After breakfast Annalise took us to the harbor and a boat that conveyed us around the southern tip of Norway and then North to the Hardanger Fjord.

<u>Another digression:</u> When Annalise got to Philadelphia, she wrote to me and accepted my invitation to a football weekend. (In

our semi-monastic life at Yale, the only recreational, co-ed relief we had in the fall was the notorious football weekends. Incidentally, Yale had an excellent team that year.) Annalise enjoyed our tour of the campus and liked the game even more. She had never seen a football game and on the bus out to Yale Bowl complained that she probably would not understand it. I told her not to worry.

After we reached our seats in the student section of the Yale Bowl, I explained that the guys in blue were the good guys; those in red were the baddies. The object of the game for each team is to get the football across the opponent's goal line. So, for us, when the ball moves toward the goal line that the reds are protecting, we are nappy; but when it moves toward the other goal line we are sad. She caught on quite quickly, and soon she was loudly and enthusiastically cheering the Yalies on. We won the game. We exchanged a few letters later, but it dwindled off, and I never saw her again. I assume she returned to Oslo after the year with her uncle was up.

To return to our tour, again. There was a quiet majesty to the Hardanger Fjord, which we enjoyed and photographed.

Hardanger Fjord

When we landed, we boarded two buses and started riding up one of the mountains. What a trip. We were on a single-lane, twisting road, which most of the time was running closely along the edge of a cliff, beyond which was a drop of over a thousand feet,

After about an hour working our way up the mountain, we noticed still higher up, another bus wending its way down toward us on this narrow mountain road. For about ten minutes we kept getting closer, at about forty miles per hour. Silently, we all wondered how two buses could possibly pass each other on this single-lane road. You could feel the rising tension among us when our buses did not even seem to be slowing down. Suddenly the road widened to two lanes and with none of the buses slowing down, the down-bound bus blew its horn as it whizzed by our two up-bound buses. Then the road narrowed back to one lane as we proceeded on up the mountain. I heard a voice from the back of our bus, "Whew! I'm sure glad these buses run on schedule," followed by a burst of nervous laughter.

About an hour farther up the mountain we came to a small village called Voss. This was a picture-book setting alongside a lake with more mountain peaks rising in the background.

Voss

The townspeople greeted us enthusiastically. Their connection to America was that Knute Rockne, the famous football player and later legendary coach at Notre Dame, was a favorite son of Voss, and they were obviously proud of him – rightfully so.

The village had only one building large enough for our concert, a large, barn-like structure, obviously used for all kinds of gatherings. In it, first we were treated to a fine dinner, prepared and served by young ladies and women of the village. After dinner, we were led to a smaller side room where we found our bags, and we were told to dress for the evening's concert.

When we returned to the main room where we had dined, it had been transformed into a concert hall, with risers set up at one end, faced by rows of chairs and benches for an audience. The people, too, had changed, from every-day casual clothes into dressier ones. The women and girls particularly were a breath-taking sight, wearing beautiful, multicolored dresses. We thought of them as native costumes.

Voss - Glee Clubbers and dancing girls

Our concert, we were told, was to be different. We started without the usual printed programs. Instead, Barty would announce each number as we went along. We had already learned that most people in Norway also spoke and understood English, having been taught it as early as grammar school.

After several numbers we had an intermission when we mingled with the audience as we enjoyed light refreshments. We were then asked to sit in the audience area while eighteen or twenty of the younger ladies moved to the front and performed songs and danced for us all, earning raucous cheers and clapping from the Glee Club members.

We returned to the risers and moved into the more familiar parts of our standard program, winding up with a couple of numbers where the audience joined in with us. It was an evening of joy for us, and obviously, also for the residents of Voss, who joined us after the concert in another part of the building for still more eating, drinking, and singing.

We finally returned to the main "concert" room and found that some of the men had cleared the room and placed along the walls a series of mattresses. At the foot of each mattress was a blanket and pillow. In this large room we all were to get a good night's sleep.

The next morning, we reboarded our two buses and continued on up the mountain, finally stopping at what appeared to be a resort. It was beautiful and seemed to be a ski center in the winter. There was still, in July, some snow on the ground, but not enough for skiing. We had three to four hours of relaxation.

After dinner (no concert today) we spent the night there and in the morning we got back on the buses, took another one-laned road that led forever downward, and ended up next to a ship in Oslo harbor. The ship took us back to Copenhagen where, after a couple of hours waiting in a railroad station, we were gathered in a group and told a bit about the next phase of our tour.

From there, we were led toward the train tracks, past the usual platforms, to two railroad cars resting on a siding. Barty announced,

"We are about to enter Germany. Because where we are going there will be no usable hotel facilities, these two cars will be your home for the next two weeks."

We then boarded the cars, which were well built and adequately furnished, and we picked out our sleeping bunks, some upper, some lower. Soon after, near dark, we felt a bump and the cars started to move. We had been attached to a regular train, which fortunately had a dining car that we visited for dinner. The next morning, we woke up in Kassel, Germany.

GERMANY

A little background is in order. At the Yalta Conference before the end of the war, Roosevelt, Churchill, and Stalin agreed that after the war, control of Germany would be divided among the big powers. Russia was to get the eastern zone, and the western zone would be divided, for purposes of interim government, into three zones controlled respectively, by the U.S., England, and France.

Berlin was to be special. The city was located in the Russian Zone, but it was to be governed in a similar, partitioned way, and the Russians were to allow free access by the western nations to and from Berlin.

In general, they actually worked it out as they had agreed. By the summer of 1949, however, disputes had arisen between Russia and the three western nations. The U.S.-controlled part of Germany, had for its leader John J. McCloy. He loved music, had a great sense of humor, and also was an accomplished pianist. They called him "High Commissioner for the American Zone." In that capacity, he had earlier worked out with Barty the plan to add two weeks in Germany to our planned four-week tour of western Europe and Scandinavia. We would travel in, and live in, two large, Pullman-type railroad cars, which could be attached to various trains and then dropped off at railroad sidings in the cities that we would visit. We were to perform fifteen concerts in fourteen days, with each day at a different university city, beginning in Berlin and ending up in Heidelberg. The purpose, according to McCloy, was a kind of good will tour, where we would primarily meet with and mingle with the students at the various universities.

While we were in the Scandinavia phase of our tour, the Russians closed down Berlin and refused to permit any water, food, or other supplies to be shipped in to the western sectors. They did allow passenger traffic in and out of the city. The western allies responded by setting up an airlift, hundreds of DC 3's flying in and out, on a 24/7 basis, supplying the western sectors of Berlin with the essentials of life. It was almost entirely a U.S. operation.

So, that was the political situation going on at the time we left Copenhagen for Kassel. In retrospect, it looks like it was an early sign of the soon-to-be-developed Cold War with Russia that lasted to the 1980s.

Our two cars of sleeping Glee Clubbers were dropped off during the night on a railroad siding in Kassel, a city of about 75,000 people, that had been a major railroad center for Germany. It also had a manufacturing plant for the Nazi's Tiger Tanks. Because of its importance to the Nazi war effort, the allies had bombed the city forty times during the war.

We woke up early in the morning and went outside our cars to get our first look at Germany. We looked around but could not see a single building standing, even though they told us we were located near the center of the city. It was nothing but rubble, with streets cleared through it. There had been so much destruction from the bombing that even now, four years after the end of the war, in this Russian zone city, all the people were still living underground in their roofed-over basements.

Kassel – current. Compare with Kassel in 1949

Kassel in 1949

A train picked up our two cars and took us into Berlin, about twenty miles away. While we were in Berlin we were treated to a bus tour around the city. Of course, there was a lot of rubble left from the bombings. But we could freely travel back and forth into and out of the Russian sector. (This was before the Berlin wall was erected.)

Berlin – Brandenburg Gate

In the afternoon we were to give an outdoor, garden concert at the American Embassy., which was directly below the flight path of the planes taking off as part of the airlift.

Every 90 seconds a plane would fly over at about 200 feet high, straining to gain altitude, and making it impossible for us on the ground to hear anything. For our afternoon "concert," therefore, we did our best to fill in the short gaps of silence between planes with single verses of various Yale songs. In the evening, however, we were able to give our regular concert in a real concert hall at the University of Berlin. We then returned to our railroad cars to begin our visits to the Universities in the western section of Germany.

Except for Heidelberg, the pattern was always the same. We would go to sleep in our cars, a train would hook us up for travel, and we would wake up the next morning on a siding in the next city. We would be taken to the University, perhaps do a little sight-seeing on the way, as in Munich and Frankfurt, meet a group of students, be shown around the university, have dinner, give a concert, and get in our cars for the trip to the next city. Our goal was to be ambassadors of goodwill for the university people, and especially the students.

While in Germany we sang concerts at the Berlin, University oof

Marburg, Theater in Offenbach, University of Frankfurt, Town Gall in Gessen, Augsburg Opera House, University of Munich, University of Erlangen, Stuttgart Opera House, and the schloss at Heidelberg.

University of Marburg

University of Tubingen

We. came to appreciate our nylon clothing while living in these two cars for two weeks. Of course, there was no laundry facility available to us. But we found that we could easily wash our shirts, socks, and underwear in the one basin in each car. Once washed clean, the clothes would be laid out on a towel. We would roll the item up in the towel and then two of us would pull the ends of the rolled-up towel. When the towel was unrolled we had a dry item, fresh as can be. The nylon underwear did have one drawback. When singing on a hot night, such as we had on July 4th in Stockholm, you could feel beads of sweat running down your back and legs. Nylon does not absorb moisture like cotton does.

A couple of days after Berlin, Mr. McCloy met with us one evening after the concert at the Goethestrasse Theater in Offenbach. He joined us for dinner, and afterward, won us over by sitting at the piano and leading and singing with us some familiar folk songs, such as "Let me Call You Sweetheart" and "Down by the Old Mill Stream" .Then, he said he would like to make a deal with us. After the Heidelberg concert, which was supposed to end our tour, he would like to put on a command performance of the Glee Club back in Berlin. He would invite the official staffs of the Russian, French, British, and American embassies. It would mean only two extra days for us and he thought it would be a boon to relations with the Russians. He said if all the club members agreed to do this concert, he would arrange it and, as a reward, he would provide to each Glee Club member travel orders for 30 days, flying free on American military aircraft that were regularly flying throughout Europe. The entire Glee Club agreed enthusiastically.

At one of our stops we were in Geowhen, near the town of Darmstadt. We were warned not to go there. During the war, a B-17 bomber had been shot down and the crew of eight bailed out over Darmstadt. All eight were captured and then lynched by the citizens. In retaliation, the Eighth Air Force paid a special visit and completely devastated Darmstadt. Even now, four years later, the people were, perhaps understandably, resentful of Americans, so we carefully avoided the place.

Every other place we went in Germany, however, we were given friendly, even enthusiastic, receptions. The people, however, were reluctant to talk about the war. They had been Nazis but they knew nothing about the atrocities committed during the war.

Among the places we sang were the University of Marburg, University of Frankfurt, University of Augsburg, University of Munich, University of Erlangen, the opera house at Stuttgart, and the Sjloss at Heidelberg. We had a few hours of sightseeing in Munich, and I recall admiring the famous town clock there with its active, life-sized figures performing on each hour.

Munich - The Famous Clock

I have only one other special memory before Heidelberg. At the University of Tubingen, our student guide, who spoke reasonably good English, led two or three of us on a fairly lengthy tour of the campus and related facilities. At one point, he stopped and asked the time. It was 2:00 PM. Obviously upset, he said, "Oh, I missed my Hoover Lunch." We asked what he meant. He said that our former President, Herbert Hoover, was in charge of a post-war U.S. sponsored food program for the U.S. zone in Germany that provided a good noon-time meal every day to the students. It was called the "Hoover Lunch," and it was then too late to make it. Apparently, this was the only solid meal the students got during the day. We apologized profusely, because he had made this sacrifice on our behalf. To make up for it we gave him a carton of cigarettes, which were very scarce in Germany and quite valuable as currency in their economy. He was very grateful.

Heidelberg was different from our visits to the other cities. During the war, by agreement of both sides, because of the historic significance of the city and its lack of any military value, neither side bombed Heidelberg. Except for one bridge across the river, there had been no war damage at all, so it was still a quaint old Bavarian town, presided over by a medieval castle (the "Schloss"), where we gave our concert. It was located half-way up a small mountain, looking over the river.

You would expect a group of Yale students arriving at this famed historic site to eagerly jump out and tour the wonders of Heidelberg. No way. We arrived there about 10:00 in the morning and pulled into the railroad sliding. Four of us were playing bridge on the train. When asked if we were going to take a tour, we replied, "No, we would rather continue our bridge game." After six weeks, we were tired, and toured out.

There were no student-hosts for us in Heidelberg, so we were mainly on our own.

Heidelberg Castle

After the Heidelberg concert in the Heidelberg Castle, Mr. McCloy had arranged for us a special dinner. We expected to get more details about the command performance in Berlin. However, it was bad news. He told us that the Russian group had refused to come and since they were the primary reason for having the concert, there would be no command performance. However, he said, because we had been so willing and cooperative and had done such a great job during the two weeks, he would provide each of us with the free travel orders for two weeks, although he could not do it for a full month.

Most of the Glee Clubbers took good advantage of this opportunity for free travel around Europe. Indeed, back in school in September we learned that two members had discovered that when they wandered onto an air base saying that they had travel orders from John McCloy, no one looked closely at them. They just told them where the next few planes were heading and told them "Hop aboard the one you want." So they flew on those two-week orders for the remaining six weeks of the Summer.

THE TRIP HOME

Unfortunately, I was unable to do this, because I had received word that my sister was getting married, and I had to return to the States for the wedding, which I did the next day. One other singer, Jerry, was, like me, going home immediately. We boarded one of Pan Am's Lockheed Airliners at Frankfurt and headed west on a beautiful sunny day. The sky was blue and cloudless. As we neared the North American coast, the Captain sent a stewardess to invite us into the cockpit. He told me to sit in the co-pilot's seat and pointed out Boston and Cape Cod far below us and to our right. What an experience. I thanked him for his courtesy.

We landed at LaGuardia Airport, which back then still handled international flights. As Jerry and I descended to the tarmac we saw Jerry's parents, who had come to meet him. I had told Jerry that I had a problem – I had completely run out of cash and did not know how I was going to get to my reserved flight back to Corning. Jerry explained this to his father who immediately offered to give me the necessary cash. I declined the offer with thanks, but told him I would be grateful if he would lend me $220.00 for the trip. He willingly agreed.

My flight to the Chemung County Airport had one stop, in Ithaca, at the south end of Seneca Lake, the longest of New York's Finger Lakes. Without cash, I had been unable to call ahead for someone to meet me, so when we landed, I took my bag and started to hitchhike for the six miles to my home in corning. An obliging driver picked me up and after inquiring about my trip, deposited me right in front of my house, where I was gleefully welcomed.

Corning, NY

After the wedding, I spent three lazy weeks at Lake Keuka and then struck off, back to New Haven, to begin my senior at Yale.

Yale in 1949

Post Script: During the school year, a men's chorus from the University of Oslo came to New Haven as part of a singing tour. The few of us who had been on the summer's tour thought that we should give them an appropriate welcome when they came to perform at Yale's Woolsey Hall. We prepared both the Yale Glee Club and the Apollo Glee Club. On the night of the concert we gathered in Woolsey Hall's Second Balcony and when the University of Oslo Singers came onto the stage, we met them with a four-part arrangement of the Norwegian National Anthem. They all stood at attention and at the end, they cheered us. Later, we entertained them with a post-concert dinner.

RETROSPECTION

Looking back on this 1949 European Tour of the Yale Glee Club from today's perspective seventy-five years later, it would be nice to be able to say that the tour had a significant impact on international relations, or on the development of choral singing in Europe, or even in some specific university in the post-war era. But such rewarding thoughts do not spring to mind. I can't even claim that the life of a single European was changed by our efforts there.

I can, however, assert with confidence that the lives of sixty-five young men from Yale were significantly altered by the trip. For most of us, our view of a world recovering from World War II was broadened, our understanding of the significance of different cultures was deepened, and our grasp of the difficulties created by different languages was heightened.

We also became keenly aware of how fortunate we in the United States were to have been spared the ravages and destruction suffered by the European nations during World War II. Through the trip we became keenly aware of how important the generosity of our

Marshall Plan was in assisting other people and nations to recover and rebuild after the war's devastation.

In a very real sense, the 1949 European Trip made me proud to be an American.

George C. Pratt

APPENDIX

From the Class of 1949 the following men (Seniors) were members of the Yale Glee Club:

Thomas C. Babbitt, G. Michael bache, M. Brewster Barton, Channing P. Baxter, Basil B. Beeken, James R. Blanning, Sevier Bonnie, Jr., George Bremser, Jr., Walter S. Browning, William H. Bunn, Jr., William Sloane Coffin, Clive Lyon Dill, Jr., William A. Edmonds, R. Kemmerer Edwards, John E. Eustis, William Y. Gard, R. Phillip Barnes, Jr., Karl R. Jacobson, William T. Leonard, Jr., Robert L. Lewis, David McCord Lippincott, J. Thomas McAndrew, Iver C. Macdougall, Jr., Richard Mather Mapes, J. Rodney Meredith, Claarke K. Oler, Arthur I. Palmer, Jr., Otis A. Pease, Stephen Potter, Frank W. Price, H. Leonard Richardson, Jr., Richard S. Rothschild, David E. Schreiber, C. Philip Skardon, Eric C. Sundean, Horace D. Taft, Edward N. Thompson, Jay W. Tracey, Jr., William M. Wagner, Lee McDowell Wagy, William H. Willis, Jr., Benjamin Wright, and Bradford Wright.

The following men, from different classes, were added to the Glee Club for the European Tour:

Walter Collins, Steven Harbachek, Fenno Heath, and George Pratt.

ACKNOWLEDGMENTS

This book would not have been possible without the contributions of three people. First, my wife, Susanah Pratt. It was her curiosity about the Glee Club's EuropeanTour that stimulated my memories of those seventy-year-old events and led me to write about them. Also, her questions about certain matters helped me focus on the details. Finally, her invaluable assistance in editing and proofreading greatly improved the final product.

Second, I need to recognize the assistance of Sean T. Maher who so willingly offered to help in my search for information in the Glee Club archives about the 1949 tour. He produced for the book the photo of the 1949 Glee Club. His assistance was most appreciated.

Third, the influence and leadership of Marshall Bartholomew and his role in building the solid reputation of the Yale Glee Club cannot be ignored. Barty was a leader in developing international choral singing, and it was that role that provided him with the friends and contacts around the world that opened doors for the concerts and welcoming celebrations for each tour abroad.

Without the contributions of these three, this book could never have been written.

ABOUT THE AUTHOR

George C. Pratt was born and raised in Corning, New York, a small upstate city in western New York State. After attending Yale University and Yale Law School and after serving a clerkship with a Judge of the New York State Court of appeals, he entered law practice onLong Island as a law firm associate. After six years, he formed his own firm, which over the years has grown to over eighty lawyers.

In 1976 President Gerald Ford appointed him as a Federal District Judge and in 1982 President Ronald Reagan appointed him to the Second Circuit Court of Appeals, where he served for about 13 years. After retirement in 1985 he became a law professor at Touro Law Center, after which he served 20 years as an independent arbitrator and mediator.

As a judge and arbitrator, he did a considerable amount of writing, but seldom of published works. This book about his participation in the Yale Glee Club's 1949 European Tour is the first book he has written, although he did write a foreword for a book his father, Hon. George W. Pratt, had written about his brief experience as an upstate D.A.

Now, at age 96, he is considering another book about some of the interesting cases he presided over as a U. S. District judge.

www.ingramcontent.com/pod-product-compliance
Lightning Source LLC
Chambersburg PA
CBHW051831160426
43209CB00006B/1123